weblinks

You don't need a computer to use this book. But, for readers who do have access to the Internet, the book provides links to recommended websites which offer additional information and resources on the subject.

You will find weblinks boxes like this on some pages of the book.

weblinks

For more information on the bombing of Dresden, go to www.waylinks.co.uk /worldwarshomefront

waylinks.co.uk

To help you find the recommended websites easily and quickly, weblinks are provided on our own website, **waylinks.co.uk.** These take you straight to the relevant websites and save you typing in the Internet address yourself.

Internet safety

↗ Never give out personal details, which include: your name, address, school, telephone number, email address, password and mobile number.

↗ Do not respond to messages which make you feel uncomfortable – tell an adult.

↗ Do not arrange to meet in person someone you have met on the Internet.

↗ Never send your picture or anything else to an online friend without a parent's or teacher's permission.

↗ If you see anything that worries you, tell an adult.

A note to adults
Internet use by children should be supervised. We recommend that you install filtering software which blocks unsuitable material.

Website content

The weblinks for this book are checked and updated regularly. However, because of the nature of the Internet, the content of a website may change at any time, or a website may close down without notice. While the Publishers regret any inconvenience this may cause readers, they cannot be responsible for the content of any website other than their own.

HODDER
Wayland

The
Home Front
in
World War II

Pat Levy

HODDER
Wayland

An imprint of Hodder Children's Books

THE WORLD WARS

© 2003 White-Thomson Publishing Ltd

Produced for Hodder Wayland by
White-Thomson Publishing Ltd
2/3 St. Andrew's Place
Lewes
BN7 1UP

Series concept: Alex Woolf
Editor: Anna Lee
Designer: Simon Borrough
Consultant: Neil DeMarco
Maps: The Map Studio
Proofreader: Philippa Smith

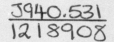

J940.531
1218908

Published in Great Britain in 2003 by Hodder Wayland, an imprint
of Hodder Children's Books.

The right of Pat Levy to be identified as the author of this work has
been asserted by her in accordance with the Copyright, Designs and
Patents Act 1988.

British Cataloguing Publication Data
Levy, Patricia, 1951-
    World War Two on the home front. (The World Wars)
    1. World War, 1939-1945 - social aspects - Great Britain -
    Juvenile literature 2. Great Britain - History - George VI,
    1936-1952 - Juvenile literature
    I. Title II. Lee, Anna
    941'.084
ISBN 0 7502 4024 5

Printed in Hong Kong.

Hodder Children's Books
A division of Hodder Headline Limited
338 Euston Road, London NW1 3BH

Picture Acknowledgements
AKG 7, 9, 10-11, 19, 28, 38, 40,
45, 57; Black Star 31; Corbis 53,
59; Hodder Wayland Picture
Library 13, 55; Hulton Getty 17;
Peter Newark Historical Pictures 8;
Peter Newark Military Pictures
4-5, 12, 16, 22, 23, 25, 27, 32,
35, 39, 41, 42, 43, 46-47, 49, 52,
54; Popperfoto 6, 15 (bottom), 21,
47, 50, 56; Topham Picturepoint
14-15, 51; TRH 58-59.

Cover photograph: Workmen
clearing the bomb site at Cannon
Street, London (The Hulton
Archive).

Contents

CHAPTER ONE

Home Fronts Across the World

The twentieth century was the century of 'total war'. This means that in times of war, war took up all the resources and manpower of the countries involved. People were killed indiscriminately in the name of war – soldiers, civilians, children, the sick, rich and poor alike. Before this, wars were generally fought between professional soldiers, usually away from areas with large civilian populations. Total war led to the idea of the 'home front' – a place where ordinary citizens worked towards the war effort and experienced the horrors of war first-hand.

World War I (1914-1918) saw the first conscription of all able-bodied men in the warring countries and the first home fronts where people not connected with the armed services had to participate in the war effort. Vast numbers of civilians came under attack by the enemy and had to defend their own towns and villages from invasion. World War II (1939-45) saw much greater involvement from the ordinary citizens of the countries involved. It is estimated that 85 million people died during World War II, perhaps 60 million of them civilians.

Some figures for numbers of civilians and soldiers killed during World War II

	Civilians	Soldiers
Britain	100,000	264,000
China	7,750,000	2,050,000
European Jews	6,000,000	
Germany	750,000	3,500,000
India	1,500,000-3,000,000	24,000
Japan	1,000,000	600,000
Poland	5,500,000	120,000
USA	6,000	320,000
USSR	7,000,000	11,000,000
Yugoslavia	1,200,000	300,000

Many more millions of people, both soldiers and civilians, died in the battlefields and home fronts of Asia, the Middle East, Africa and the Pacific.

The War Effort in Japan

Shimizu Mitsuo, an eighteen-year-old substitute teacher in a rural area of Japan, kept a war diary about her students. This excerpt from 1945, just months before Japan's surrender, shows how civilians became involved in civil defence:

8 June: early morning prayers for victory at shrine with students; practise bamboo spear attacks on shrine grounds.
11 June: cultivate school grounds and plant sweet potatoes and pumpkins. In the afternoon, transport military supplies to next village with students.
23 June: in between air raid alerts, cut wheat on the riverbank. After this practise bamboo spearing and stone throwing in the event of an enemy land invasion.
19 July: attacks by carrier based planes increase. Carried charcoal from deep in the mountains five miles away. Spurred on crying pupils by saying it was all for victory's sake...'

Frank Gibney (ed.), *Senso: The Japanese Remember the Pacific War*, East Gate, 1995.

A boy and his dog survey the ruins of their home in Hendon (north London) in May 1941.

Many millions of civilians lost their homes during the course of World War II.

The War Economy

The home fronts of World War II became as important in the struggle for power as the war fronts. All the warring powers turned the economies of their countries towards the war effort and home fronts played a vital part in keeping the war going, producing armaments, supplies, fresh troops, medical backup and a base for attacks.

The biggest battles on the home fronts were for the control of the country itself – as many as thirty countries were invaded during World War II. In many cases such countries became a part of the machinery of the enemy's war effort as their factories were turned over to the invader's needs, their food supplies were diverted to the occupying forces and their citizens conscripted into work that helped the war effort.

Civilians in the Crossfire

At different times in Europe, the troops of opposing countries fought in areas where civilian populations lived and worked. Italy became a battleground as opposing troops fought for control of the country. Around the Mediterranean, Malta, Greece, Syria, Egypt, Morocco, Algeria, Iraq and Libya were all drawn into the war. As a result of the German invasion of the USSR, civilian populations were drawn into battle as their homes were looted, commandeered or burned down. In the Pacific,

Young Japanese women working in an armaments factory. Japanese war workers laboured for long hours, often for little pay.

Countries throughout the world were affected by World War II. Here in 1943 in Algeria, the people celebrate as the occupying Italian and German troops are replaced by a liberating French army.

Japanese and American soldiers fought one another on islands such as Guadalcanal and the Marianas, where civilians were living. Those civilians living in occupied countries, especially in parts of Eastern Europe and Asia, experienced particularly harsh conditions during the period of occupation.

Civilians on the British, German, Japanese, French and Italian home fronts also endured terrible bombing raids that destroyed whole cities and left the survivors without shelter or food. Even countries far removed from the theatres of war, for example, Australia, and the United States, experienced brief attacks. Neutral countries such as Ireland were affected by the war with food shortages and bombing raids.

The invasion of Greece

In Greece civilians bore the brunt of an invasion by Italy and then invasion by German troops. The Italian invasion in 1940 was short-lived but brutal, with Italian forces entering Greece through Albania and encountering fierce resistance from Greek troops and civilians alike. The following April German troops invaded Greece and quickly drove Greek and Allied troops southwards, destroying homes and looting as they went.

During the German occupation of Greece there were uprisings by partisan groups of all political persuasions, but their failure sometimes led to terrible reprisals against local populations. For three years the people of Greece suffered food shortages, conscription, arrest and imprisonment, until the German occupation drew to an end in 1944.

CHAPTER TWO

Bombing Civilians

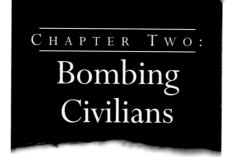

Bombing Britain

When the war began in 1939, both Britain and Germany were reluctant to carry out bombing attacks on civilian targets and for the first few months of the war both countries focused on the enemy's ports and air force bases. In August 1940, the first German bombs were dropped on London, but they were aimed at the docks rather than civilian targets. Later, factories in the Midlands of Britain were targeted in the hope that their owners would force Churchill to make peace rather than have their factories destroyed. Coventry, Liverpool, Belfast, Plymouth, London and many other major urban centres were attacked in the initial blitz of 1940-1941, in a second wave in summer 1942 and then regularly until the end of the war.

Volunteers salvage what they can from a suburban British street. The centre house has taken a direct hit from a German bomb.

The British Hit Back

In retaliation against the German attack of August 1940, British bombers were sent to German cities with the intention of bombing indiscriminately in the hope that some military or economic targets might be hit. The British bombing campaign of Germany began in earnest in 1942 and was aimed specifically at civilian targets in an effort to demoralize the population. The British also believed that heavy bombing would force Germany to concentrate its efforts on defence rather than expanding its conquests any further. Attacks were designed to cause maximum damage, with explosive and incendiary bombs directed at densely populated areas of wooden housing in urban areas such as Berlin, Dresden, Lubeck, Rostock and Cologne. In 1943 a ten-day raid on Hamburg created fire-storms with 240 kph winds at 1,000 °c raging through the city leaving 50,000 people dead.

Three boys stand amid the ruins of Berlin in 1945. By the end of the war much of Berlin had been destroyed by Allied bombing raids.

The bombing of Dresden

By February 1945 it had become clear that the Allies would win the war, yet the British and Americans nevertheless decided to bomb the city of Dresden. Dresden had few factories that contributed to the war effort, very little in the way of shelter for its residents, and large areas of wooden housing. In addition, because it was late into the war, the city population was swelled by thousands of refugees fleeing the Soviet invasion from the east. An estimated 70-80,000 people died in Dresden in one night.

weblinks

For more information on the bombing of Dresden, go to **www.waylinks.co.uk/worldwarshomefront**

Bombing Japan

In the early years of World War II Japan was immune to aerial attack because it was so far from American bases. By 1944 US troops had captured Saipan, an island in the central Pacific, and American aircraft could reach Tokyo.

US planes did not concentrate on attacking Japan's strategic military targets. Instead they carpet bombed cities. Japan was losing the war and there was little air raid provision and few resources to help its citizens. Forty per cent of Osaka and 50 per cent of Tokyo, Kobe and Yokohama were destroyed and a quarter of a million people died. Evacuation plans were slow to come into place and shelters were only constructed in 1944.

Japan was given the opportunity to surrender in the early summer of 1945, but despite the suffering of its citizens its government responded by calling into military service all men and women aged between fifteen and forty. As a result, the USA decided to drop an atomic bomb on Hiroshima, a city of 320,000 people. Three days later a second, larger bomb was dropped on Nagasaki, killing 70,000 people immediately and thousands more in the days and years that followed. The USA was prepared to build more such bombs and use them on other cities, but on 2 September 1945 Japan surrendered. In the meantime the incendiary attacks on Tokyo had continued, dropping twelve million tons of explosives and incendiary bombs and killing tens of thousands of people.

Air Raids Across the Globe

French and Italian civilians also experienced terrible bombing raids that destroyed whole cities and left the survivors without shelter or food. Even neutral countries, such as the Republic of Ireland, experienced accidental bombing attacks when German bombers mistook their targets.

On the night of 9 March 1945, American bombers attacked Tokyo, leaving nearly 125,000 dead or injured and over a million homeless.

weblinks

For more information on the bombing of Hiroshima, go to
www.waylinks.co.uk/worldwars homefront

Hiroshima

The atomic bomb fell at 8.16 a.m. as people were beginning their day. It exploded 609.6 metres above the city and instantly destroyed 70,000 of the city's 76,000 buildings and everyone in them. The immediate death toll was between 105,000 and 125,000 people. Within 310 m of the explosion 90 per cent of all life was exterminated, with bodies leaving behind only their shadows. Further than 620 m out all soft tissue evaporated. 1.24 km away skin boiled before the blast wave ripped it off. Further away people didn't die but wandered about, mutilated and in agony.

Air Raid Provision

When war began both Britain and Germany began to make provision for the thousands of civilians who would inevitably experience mass bombing raids. In Britain the public were issued with gas masks and children were evacuated to the countryside. After the first air raids on London, people began to take shelter in underground stations for the duration of the raid, which made travel by Underground impossible. At first conditions were terrible, but eventually the stations became better organized, with special passes for a place in each station, bunk beds, kitchens and toilets. Tickets for places were sold on the black market and 177,000 people sheltered in 80 stations each night.

A Night in the Underground

George Martin, an air raid warden, remembers a night he had to spend in one of the underground stations in London:

'I do not know how many people were down there, it was cold, the ground was wet with water and it was dark. I used my torch to find my way through, and I could see people huddled together, they seemed like tramps or gypsies to me. They were unclean, and stank. I almost felt sick, and my stomach turned over ... Where was the pride of these people, how could they live like this? I felt ashamed that these people were Londoners the same as I was.'

George Martin, quoted on www.battleofbritain.net

Aldwych tube station in the West End of London. This part of the Underground was converted into a permanent bomb shelter for the duration of the war, and housed art treasures as well as civilians.

In the rest of the country Anderson shelters were distributed – these were sheets of corrugated iron that were half buried in back gardens. In the event of an air raid one or two families crowded into the shelter, which was often flooded, unheated and damp. Another form of shelter was the Morrison shelter, a steel table kept inside the house under which a family could huddle during air raids. The big hotels such as the Dorchester and Savoy in London opened their basements to their wealthy customers and offered a floor show and meal along with the night's shelter.

Germany was far better organized than Britain for the bombing raids. Preparations for air attack in Germany had begun in 1935 and by the time the bombs actually started to fall Germany was protected by a million men operating anti-aircraft guns. Bomb shelters were prepared in 82 cities, either in cellars or in purpose built towers and deep bunkers. They contained emergency water and food supplies, and outside each city more supplies were ready to support the survivors of any attack.

American troops in front of an air raid shelter in Aachen, Germany. It was able to hold thousands of people during a bombing raid.

CHAPTER THREE

Occupation and Resistance

People living in countries that were invaded by enemy forces often had to stand by and watch as troops marched into their towns, took what they wanted, burned what was not needed and moved on. Millions of people's lives descended into chaos as food stores were stripped, farms destroyed and thousands of people were deported or fled.

weblinks

For more information on the siege of Leningrad go to **www.waylinks.co.uk/worldwars homefront**

The Siege of Leningrad

In 1941 German troops moved into the Soviet Union, and in August they reached the outskirts of Leningrad. About 2.8 million people lived in the city and, as the troops approached, no attempt was made to evacuate them. For 890 days German troops besieged the city. By October people were beginning to starve. Strict rationing was imposed by the Soviet authorities but for most people all that was available was about 125 grams of bread per day. People began to freeze to death in the coldest winter in living memory as the electricity supply failed and sources of fuel ran out. Cannibalism came into practice and about 300 people were executed for the crime. Approximately 650,000 people died before the first winter of the siege ended and the authorities were able to evacuate civilians and bring food to those who remained. By January 1944, when the siege was broken, only 600,000 people remained in the city.

An emaciated man holds his daily bread ration during the Siege of Leningrad, 1941-44.

Occupation in Europe

In Western Europe, Germany invaded many neighbouring countries, including France, Holland, Belgium, Denmark, Poland, Czechoslovakia and Austria, which spent the war years as occupied countries with German laws imposed on them. Their economies became geared to helping the German war machine and, in some cases, civilians were taken to Germany to work in German industries. Most civilians experienced food shortages and severe restrictions placed on their normal lives. For example, in Holland all social life came to an end as movement was restricted by law and people became completely preoccupied with daily survival.

By 1941 about 260 million people were living under German occupation. After a brief initial period of chaos when civilians fled the cities (in 1940 three million Belgians and seven million French fled their homes) some people were able to carry on with their lives in relative peace. Many others suffered terribly during occupation, and thousands lost their lives.

Citizens of Warsaw, Poland, survey the damage to their city as Germans move in to occupy their city in September 1939.

Life Under Occupation

During the German occupation of Holland, petrol, food and fuel were drastically rationed until poorer people were living on around 1,000 calories a day. Floorboards and furniture were burned to keep families warm and thousands of men were drafted into the war industries in Germany. Wherever German control was threatened there were terrible reprisals – in France even low-level resistance efforts were met with mass murders while in Greece whole villages were wiped out. As families were separated and people struggled to find enough food and shelter, daily life became a battle for survival.

Northern Europe

In northern European countries such as Denmark the lives of civilians were determined by Nazi ideology. The citizens of these countries (with the obvious exception of the Jewish citizens) were considered 'Aryan' and therefore worthy of a place in the greater German state, which would come into existence when the war was over. Consequently every effort was taken to make the

Paris, 14 June 1940. German troops take over the city of Paris as shocked Parisians look on. This was to be the beginning of four years of occupation.

occupation as acceptable as possible and to re-educate the population in Nazi ideals. As the war progressed and the need for resources grew, this policy gradually took second place as greater demands were placed on the citizens of the occupied countries.

Settling the Score

Collaborators – people who for cynical or political reasons chose to work with the occupying forces against their own people – existed in all the occupied countries in Europe. In many instances collaborators were hated even more than the occupying troops. When liberation came in France, there was a massive urge to seek justice against those who had collaborated with the Germans. At first this took the form of a 'rough justice' – perhaps as many as 10,000 collaborators were attacked and murdered. Later, formal trials were held and less vindictive sentences such as prison terms were passed against the collaborators. One group of people who were singled out were women who had formed relationships with German soldiers. These women were often dragged out of their homes by their neighbours to have their hair shaved off in the street. In Paris this was jokingly referred to as *la coiffure de '44* – the hairstyle of 1944. Later such relationships were not included in the list of crimes committed by collaborators.

German troops occupied Denmark from 1940 until the end of the war in 1945. They met increasingly stubborn resistance in the form of sabotage, illegal newspapers, strikes and a determination to protect Jewish people. Here a Danish collaborator is being taken to face trial soon after the German troops surrendered in May 1945.

Occupied Poland

Polish civilians suffered particularly during World War II. Their country was invaded by both Germany and the Soviet Union in 1939. In German-occupied Poland civilians were considered racially inferior (*untermenschen*) because of their Slavic ethnic origins. They were therefore not worthy to live as German citizens and no attempt was made to assimilate them into wider German society. The Nazi plan was to eliminate the *untermenschen* population in order to create *lebensrum* (living space) for Germans. Terror and hunger dominated the lives of the Poles who survived. First the intellectuals, then the Polish underground, then ordinary people were arrested and deported to German slave camps. About 200,000 children were taken from their families to be raised in Germany. All Polish men of suitable age were forcibly drafted into the German army. Between October 1943 and July 1944 an average of 300 people were shot each week in the streets of Warsaw for offences as minor as black marketeering.

Some fortunate Poles managed to escape before the German invasion. Here two children join a chain of refugees carrying their belongings on horses and in carts.

The fate of Polish people in Soviet occupied territory was little better. More than a million people were deported to other parts of the Soviet Union, including Siberia, and an estimated 80 per cent of the deportees died as a result of the hardships associated with transportation, such as malnutrition and disease. During the Soviet occupation, 200,000 Poles were conscripted into the Soviet army. It is estimated that by the end of the war as many as 20 per cent of Poland's pre-war population had died.

Auschwitz

Some areas of German-occupied Poland were used first of all to house deported Jews and then to create death camps where Europe's Jews were sent to be gassed or worked to death. One such area was near Auschwitz, a town in southern Poland. Auschwitz was chosen because of its rail links with most of the major cities of Europe. The first Jews were sent to the camp in 1942 and in the same year a second camp, Birkenau, was set up nearby. At first the gassings took place in a converted farmhouse but later gas chambers and crematoria for the disposal of the bodies were built. Over the next two years the work camp grew until it was providing slave labour for factories built around it in satellite camps. By August 1944 Auschwitz was killing 20,000 people a day: Jews, Soviet and Polish prisoners of war, homosexuals, Jehovah's Witnesses, communists and gypsies.

These children were among those left behind at Auschwitz when German guards abandoned the camp in 1945. In the chaos of the final weeks of the camp they had escaped the initial selections that usually resulted in the deaths of all children.

weblinks↖

For more information on the Auschwitz concentration camp, go to **www.waylinks.co.uk/worldwars homefront**

Japanese Occupation in Asia

A number of countries, including Thailand, Malaya, Burma, China and the Philippines, were invaded by the Japanese and became occupied territories. At the height of its power Japan controlled large areas of China and South-east Asia. Like Germany, it hoped to exploit its new territories' natural resources. At first many of the countries it occupied welcomed the Japanese troops as liberators from their imperial powers – Britain, the USA, Holland and France – but it quickly became clear that the Japanese intention was to replace Europeans rather than to create independent states. Japanese policy towards the native people was considerably worse than their treatment of captured Western civilians.

Before World War II began, Japan had invaded China, killing tens of thousands of Chinese civilians in the Nanjing massacre in 1937. The mass killing of civilians continued as they invaded Malaya, Indochina and Indonesia. Chinese people who had settled in Malaya and Indonesia generations before were considered to be the enemies of Japan and were indiscriminately murdered in their thousands. Little attention was paid to whether they represented a genuine threat and even children, women, the old and the sick were massacred. Thousands of civilians were sent on marches to work in slave camps and on the Thai-Burma railway. Women, particularly Koreans, were drafted into camps where they became 'comfort women', forced to provide sex for Japanese soldiers.

The Japanese invade Malaya

At the same time as Japan attacked Pearl Harbor in Hawaii, Japanese troops were making their way through Malaya, driving the British before them. Ismail Mohammed Amin, who was twenty years old at the time, remembers what it was like:

'I was 20, fresh out of school when I heard that the Japanese forces had invaded Malaya. I was in Singapore, working with the Ministry of Education then … Rumours abounded about the atrocities and brutalities committed by them [the Japanese] even before the war had begun. Soon after [the invasion], I left for Malaya by hitching a ride on a goods train leaving from Singapore to Tampin. When I arrived in Malacca town, I saw severed heads of some locals placed on stakes at several junctions in the town. It was a great shock to me.'

weblinks

For more information on the Nanjing massacre go to **www.waylinks.co.uk/worldwarshomefront**

People who were not targeted for death or slavery nevertheless suffered many hardships in their daily lives. Food became scarce, they were forced into humiliating shows of deference towards the occupying forces and most families who could do so hid their women in the countryside.

Burmese refugees take what they can carry and flee from the Japanese into territory still held by British forces. Burmese civilians were caught up in the Japanese invasion during 1941 and 1942 and Burma (now called Myanmar) was occupied by the Japanese until 1944.

The massacre at Sandakan

In 1943 the Japanese army entered the tiny town of Sandakan on the island of Borneo. All Europeans were taken away and imprisoned in camps and many local civilians were forced into labour, building an airstrip and other works aimed at the war effort. The area remained relatively peaceful until 1945 when American planes bombed Sandakan and American boats docked for a short time in its harbour. Local people went out to meet the Americans and, as a reprisal, leading Chinese businessmen and community leaders from the town were taken to the Japanese headquarters and murdered. Later the Japanese burned the town to the ground as they departed.

Resistance

While the vast majority of civilians buckled down to life under occupying powers, others chose to resist. Resistance took many forms. At the simplest level it might have been doing one's work as badly as possible so as to harm the war effort, listening to the banned BBC broadcasts or celebrating national holidays in the face of German bans. More dangerous activities including publishing newsletters, supporting or even joining armed resistance groups hiding out in the countryside, attacking occupying forces and aiding Allied soldiers and Jewish refugees in their escape. Even small acts of defiance took enormous courage, especially in the early years of the war when there seemed to be little hope of liberation. People who were discovered faced torture and death.

Holland

In Holland a little over a thousand people joined active partisan groups. For the most part people's efforts were isolated and were aimed chiefly at providing food and assistance to men in hiding from conscription. Others protected Jewish families; by 1943 about 25,000 Jews were being sheltered by the Dutch underground. The production and distribution of a secret anti-Nazi newspaper, *Trouw*, required a greater degree of organization. The paper reported news of conscriptions, food shortages and the activities of the Dutch government in exile. During the Nazi occupation, 120 people involved in distributing it were caught and executed.

The Dutch resistance movement operated throughout the German occupation. This gun was smuggled from one operation to another inside a hollowed-out book.

France

In France a network of people created an underground escape route for Jews into Spain. The route led through the countryside, avoiding main roads, with safe houses where escaping Jews could be hidden overnight by sympathetic locals. Thirty thousand people escaped occupied France via this route. Active partisan groups also operated in France, carrying out small-scale sabotage such as damaging factories, blocking roads or stealing from the occupying forces. Carrying out these small acts of resistance could result in terrible reprisals. In July 1944 resistance groups in Grenoble occupied a hill outside the city in expectation that the Allied invasion of France would soon begin and they would be relieved. The anticipated relief didn't arrive, and after two days 1,000 members of the resistance were killed without achieving anything.

Poland

Perhaps because of the particularly harsh treatment of the Polish people, resistance here was much stronger than in other countries. Ordinary people flouted regulations, teams of teenagers put up nationalistic posters and tore down those of the occupying powers. The resistance movement established schools for Polish children, set up courts, ran secret newspaper presses and financed the reopening of the University of Warsaw. Finally, on 1 August 1944, as German troops were being driven back across Poland, an uprising took place in Warsaw. The German response was savage – 200,000 civilians were killed and thousands more were deported. The expected relief by the Soviet army did not come and in October the uprising ended in complete failure.

Paris, August 1944. This French resistance group holds the Rue St Jacques as German troops are forced out of the city by invading Allied forces.

The Jews of Europe

By 1941 most of Europe's Jews were under the control of Nazi Germany. Arrangements were made to identify and isolate Jewish populations, to strip them of their possessions and jobs and to transport them to the ghettos of Poland. There they were worked, starved and then shipped on to death camps where they were murdered. Throughout Europe, the Nazi plan to round up all of Europe's Jews was met with varying degrees of co-operation or resistance.

In France the Vichy government passed anti-Semitic laws and rounded up its Jews. Austria did the same, while Belgium allowed first its foreign Jews to be deported, and later its own Jewish citizens. Dutch Jews were deported, although many thousands were kept hidden throughout the war by their neighbours. Finland and Denmark refused to allow deportations. Once the Danish government and civilians were unable to prevent the capture of Jews, most of Denmark's Jews were taken to safety in Sweden. Italy, too, refused to give up its Jews until it was occupied by Germany and even then thousands of people risked their lives to shelter as many Jews as possible. In Bulgaria farmers threatened to lie down on the tracks in front of the transport trains until its government stopped deportations. Hungary did not give up its Jews until the country was occupied by the Nazis.

These German Jewish refugees were among the lucky few who escaped from Germany before the war began and its borders were closed.

The price of sheltering Jews

The civilian populations of occupied countries reacted to the persecution of Jews in many different ways. Those who risked their own and their families' lives in order to protect Jews risked harsh German reprisals. In some places where hidden Jews were found, whole families were executed. One historian records that 'In 38 cases of Jews being saved by Poles … the Nazis murdered 97 Poles, including 30 women, 14 children and one infant'. The same historian records that in Bialystock alone, 343 Poles were shot for helping Jews. At the former concentration camp at Belzec in Poland, a monument records the deaths of 1,500 Poles who died there after trying to help their Jewish neighbours.

These children sit forlornly in the street of the Warsaw ghetto in 1941. Thousands of Jewish children were left to fend for themselves while their parents tried to make a living.

In Eastern Europe the Nazis found willing helpers in the cold-blooded executions of tens of thousands of Jews. Czech, Yugoslavian, Bulgarian and Greek Jews had little protection. In the German occupied British Channel Islands, British policemen, acting under orders from the authorities, helped round up the islands' Jews. Jewish people throughout Europe met their deaths in ways that it is almost impossible to comprehend – worked to death in slave labour camps, gunned down in woods outside villages, gassed in the camps, tortured, experimented on, beaten to death on the whim of a prison camp guard.

CHAPTER FOUR

The War Effort at Home

The US War Economy

All over the world the daily lives of civilians changed dramatically with the outbreak of war. The economies of occupied countries were put at the service of the occupying force and little attention was paid to the needs or future of the civilian population. In the countries that were still free to wage war, industry had to be put on a war footing. In 1940, a year before it entered the war, the USA started to commit its economy to becoming the 'Arsenal of Democracy'. War-related industries such as armaments, shipbuilding and weapons manufacture expanded rapidly, taking on women to replace conscripted men.

Industries that had been dedicated to peacetime use were converted for military purposes – car manufacturers made tanks and armoured vehicles, cruise ship builders made destroyers, garment factories made uniforms and parachutes. In farming, mining and steelworking, output doubled and more industrial plants were built in America's three years of war than had been built in the previous fifteen years. With the booming economy came wage increases and the price of goods in shops rose.

Here a woman is trained to use a lathe in a War Production and Training Centre in Washington D.C.

Britain

War-related industries also boomed in Britain. Cities such as Belfast, which had had massive unemployment during the 1930s, now saw an enormous increase in employment.

Armaments factories were built in the countryside and women without children to care for were drafted into them. As in the USA, factories producing peacetime goods became involved in war production. A government letter to shopkeepers announced: 'corsets become parachutes and chinstraps; lace curtains become sand-fly netting; golf balls become gas masks; mattresses become life jackets; saucepans become steel helmets'.

The USSR

In the USSR the war economy got off to a shaky start with the German invasion of the western territories and the resulting loss of workers and factories. Although production rose in the rest of the country, it was poorly organized – for example, not enough ammunition was produced for guns. The government also failed to make sure that normal production – of food, fuel, industrial machinery and steel – was maintained. As a result, power cuts, lack of machinery and lack of heating or food for factory workers became commonplace. Careful government planning ensured that the economy had improved by 1943, and as the German forces retreated, Soviet factories were producing 750 aircraft, 400 armoured cars, 2,500 guns and much more every week.

Leningrad 1942. During the siege of the city these children worked in an armaments factory.

Women at War

The call up of the majority of adult men meant that the workforce was seriously reduced in many countries. In the USA eight million women found jobs, increasing the percentage of women in the workplace from 25 per cent to 36 per cent. In 1941 a survey found 36 women employed in the shipbuilding industry; by 1943 there were 160,000. Prior to the war American women had been encouraged to see their sole role in life as homemakers, but now films such as *Rosie the Riveter*, about a woman shipbuilder, portrayed working in factories as glamorous and patriotic.

Germany

In Germany the number of women working in industry fell once the war had started because the government paid generous family allowances to the wives of conscripted men. It became financially and socially easier for women to stay at home. Those women who did work had their salaries deducted from the family allowance. By 1943 the loss of much of the male workforce to the military resulted in the passing of laws conscripting all women except those with small children into the labour force. Three million women registered for work, but most were able to avoid it.

weblinks

For more information on the British Home Guard, go to
www.waylinks.co.uk/worldwars homefront

Women assemble shells in a German factory.

Britain

The family allowance for wives of servicemen was not as generous in Britain as in Germany and many women were forced into the workplace. While some found employment in skilled factory work, replacing conscripted men, most women worked in more traditional roles such as secretaries, or were conscripted into the Auxiliary Territorial Service. Many cleaned barracks and hostels for homeless families or cooked in canteens. Others became part of the Land Army, taking up work in farming as the country began to grow more of its food than before the war.

weblinks

For more information on women on the British Home Front, go to **www.waylinks.co.uk/worldwars homefront**

Baby riots

In Britain the Ministry of Labour did its best to set up nurseries so that mothers could find work, but the Ministry of Health opposed the idea, concerned about epidemics and traumatized children. In 1941 there was a series of demonstrations by mothers of young children who wanted access to childcare. They took to the streets pushing children in prams and holding placards demanding work and nurseries. The tabloid newspapers labelled these demonstrations 'baby riots'.

Mothers and their children on their way to the town hall to demand access to childcare so that they can work during the war.

The USSR

In the USSR women had entered the workforce long before the war. Women, children, the elderly and even the sick had to work in order to survive. In some industries during the war 90 per cent of the workforce were women. In other countries such as Japan and Italy, the traditional view of women as homemakers was temporarily suspended as women workers became essential to the war effort.

Civil Defence

For Britain especially and for Germany later in the war, invasion by enemy forces was a serious and deadly threat and preparations were made for defence of these countries. The USA also took measures to deal with possible invasion. There were few attacks on American soil, but 10 million people were enrolled in the Office of Civilian Defense to learn how best to respond in the event of bombing raids or invasion. Many Americans also made improvized bomb shelters.

British coastlines were dotted with defensive bunkers, trenches were dug and barbed wire covered the beaches. Local invasion committees were set up and people living near the coast were issued orders to remain in their homes if invasion occurred. Road, railway station and shop signs were all taken down to confuse the enemy and it became a crime to leave a car or any other vehicle unlocked. Millions of civilians became air raid wardens, part time auxiliary nurses or volunteer firefighters. Many of these volunteers returned from a hard day's work to pull on their uniform and go out to check that people were observing the blackout or provide food and help to those bombed out of their homes.

For most of the war the likelihood of Germany being invaded was remote, so civil defence focused on dealing with bombing. Air raid wardens patrolled the streets ready to put out fires or rescue those trapped in damaged buildings. Volunteers helped organize the rehousing of survivors and distribution of luxury items such as coffee and chocolate. In 1944 the *Volkssturm* (Home Guard) was formed, but many people were reluctant to join. They feared that if they were captured by invading Allied troops they would be considered partisans and shot. Worse still was the possibility of being sent to the front line, as some Home Guard units were.

Dad's Army. Doing their best with very limited resources these men would have been Britain's last line of defence in an invasion. Here they practise various forms of camouflage.

Dad's Army

The British Home Guard consisted largely of men who for one reason or another were not in the armed forces. Because the majority of them were over the call up age of 18-40, they were known in Britain as Dad's Army. For the most part they were poorly armed and badly trained and were treated in the press as foolish. One story tells of a Home Guard group that hit upon the idea of stopping invaders by blocking the road with burning petrol. When they tried out the theory the road caught fire when the burning petrol leaked into drainage ditches setting fire to fields and the fire brigade had to be called out. By 1944 when the threat of invasion was over, the Home Guard was better trained and acted largely as auxiliary units for anti-aircraft gunners.

Monitoring the Home Front

In every aspect of the home front – resistance, suffering bomb attacks, working for the war effort, civil defence – the most important was the battle for the hearts and minds of the civilian populations. As long as the people on the home front believed that victory was possible, they would continue to work hard and endure the terrible suffering brought about by war. If they began to despair or mistrust their leaders, they would no longer be willing to make sacrifices in the name of war.

As the war unfolded, governments carefully observed public opinion and response to events. Information about the war was not always made public, especially if it might undermine people's morale and affect the war effort. Many public surveys and reports during the war, particularly in the USA and Britain, showed that a large proportion of the population had only a vague idea about what the aims of the war were.

Here a girl in Nazi uniform is shown collecting money to build youth hostels and homes, though the money actually went towards armaments. Such images helped promote the idea that the Nazi regime looked after its people, and was therefore worth fighting for.

In Britain the Ministry of Information set up an organization to monitor the feelings of the citizens, which came to be popularly known as 'Cooper's Snoopers' after the man who was in charge, Duff Cooper. A Mass Observation programme was also established to study the effects of war on the civilian population of Britain. It produced a very different picture from the traditional ideas about British civilians in war. A common idea is that the British rallied to the war effort, put aside class differences, kept up their spirits and laughed in the face of tragedy – and many did. But a more complex picture also emerges of dissatisfaction, class snobbery and incompetence existing beside the bravery and 'stiff upper lips'.

Hikers in Surrey in southern England have their identity cards checked by police. In January 1940, every resident in Britain was issued with a card and it was an offence not to carry it or show it to a policeman when asked. The card gave details of appearance, address, and each person had their own identity card number.

'Bravery was something purely negative'

This Mass Observation report that followed the first air raids on east London in September 1940 shows the real state of east Londoners at the time:

'...the press versions of life going on normally ... are grotesque. There was no bread, no electricity, no milk, no gas, no telephones. There was thus every excuse for people to be distressed... There was no understanding in the huge buildings of central London for the tiny crumbled streets of densely massed population. Here people wanted to be brave but found bravery was something purely negative, cheerless and without encouragement or prospect of success.'

Quoted in Arthur Marwick *The Home Front: The British and World War II*

Keeping up Morale

The countries involved in the war could keep fighting only with the support of civilians working in the factories, producing food or helping to run the voluntary organizations. High morale was important in maintaining a willing workforce. After Hitler's successful campaign in the west and the surrender of Western countries, German morale was very high. People believed that the war would soon be over and that Britain would surrender. German civilians ignored the British radio broadcasts of the atrocities being committed against Polish people. Then, as the invasion of the USSR in 1941 failed to have lasting success, morale began to flag. Despite the 1939 law called the Special Wartime Code, that made defeatism or suggesting that Germany might lose the war punishable by death, by 1943 Germany's failures in the Soviet Union were causing outright criticism of Hitler and the war. In contrast, other setbacks had a positive effect on morale in Germany. Bombing raids tended to focus people's anger against the enemy while rationing and the attempted assassination of Hitler in 1944 rallied civilians to the war effort.

In Britain similar swings in morale could be traced to developments in the war. The Blitz of 1941 had a positive effect on morale, initially reducing whole cities to near chaos and despair but famously bringing out determination in the face of tragedy.

Propaganda

The importance of civilian morale can be seen in the efforts of governments to destroy the enemy's morale. Both sides bombarded enemy territory with radio broadcasts that were a mixture of popular music, invented gossip and supposed war news, which reported

This 1943 poster shows a woman factory worker encouraging other women to join the workforce. The woman in this poster and others like it became known as Rosie the Riveter. Although she is a fictional character she represents the many women who took on jobs previously considered to be men's work. They collectively became known as Rosies.

that the opposing forces were losing. German broadcasts pointed out supposed losses and offers of peace that the British government was keeping from the population, while for their part the British broadcasting to Germany told invented stories of sexual scandal among the Nazi leaders. These were so outrageous that even the British Ambassador to Moscow, Sir Stafford Cripps, complained that they made the British broadcasters who invented them seem depraved.

weblinks

To view Allied propaganda posters, go to
www.waylinks.co.uk/worldwars homefront

Lord Haw Haw

A famous broadcaster of German propaganda was the Irish American Fascist sympathizer William Joyce, nicknamed Lord Haw Haw for his assumed upper class English accent. He became very popular in Britain during the period of the 'phoney war' between September 1939 and summer 1940, when there was little news coming from the British government. It is estimated that in any one day 26 per cent of the British population listened to his broadcasts and 17 per cent agreed with his assessment that the war had been stirred up by Jewish extremists.

William Joyce (Lord Haw Haw) after his arrest by Allied troops in 1945. He had a British passport so was put on trial for treason after the war and executed.

Entertainment

One way of keeping morale high during the war was to provide uplifting entertainment. In Britain radios became very important, as a source of both news and light entertainment. The government, worried about the stresses on the nation's women who were now working in factories as well as running their homes, arranged programmes such as 'Worker's Playtime', which were broadcast on factory floors.

The government also organized shows that were put on in factories, in the Underground shelters and to troops stationed in Britain. The 12-year-old Anne Shelton became a regular on the radio, singing requests for the nation and for the armed forces abroad. The American and British film industries began making highly patriotic war movies such as *Mrs Miniver* (1941), an American movie about a British family struggling on bravely throughout the bombing. Once the USA had entered the war films began to turn to the exploits of various

This cinema in Britain is showing two feature films and a film about air raids. Outside air raid wardens, nurses, fire wardens and army officers mingle with the crowd.

The newsreels

In the early years of the war German film makers were allowed to film the progress of the war. These films were shown in cinemas as newsreels before the main feature. At first the newsreels were a very popular part of the evening's entertainment, but by the end of the war, when people had grown weary of the fighting, the audience had to be compelled to watch them before they were allowed to see the main feature. Newsreels were also very important in American and British cinemas. As in Germany, they were carefully censored so that they did not harm morale. Newsreels introduced the horrors of Nazi concentration camps to audiences in Britain and the USA.

groups of soldiers and spies, but most people preferred films that took their minds off the war such as *The Maltese Falcon* (1941).

Nazi Cinema

In Germany film and radio also took on a propaganda role. Goebbels, the German propaganda minister, recognized the danger of a boring and war-oriented radio service – German civilians were tuning in to British radio both for news and entertainment. Popular films of the time were a mixture of musical comedy such as *Wiener Blut* (Vienna Blood) about the Congress of Vienna, and virulent anti-Jewish propaganda such as *Jud Suss* (The Jew Suss, 1940) about a wicked rich Jew who tries to corrupt a beautiful and innocent young girl. Other 'documentary' films such as *Der Ewige Jude* (The Eternal Jew, 1940) portrayed Jews as a disease that must be erased from civilized society. And yet during Hitler's time in power 1,094 feature films were made, 48 per cent of which were comedies.

Secrets and Spies

Most governments were concerned both with preventing possible enemy agents or 'fifth columnists' from discovering information and with controlling gossip and rumour. Potential enemies of the state were interned, including in Britain Jewish refugees. In addition campaigns were carried out warning people that 'careless talk costs lives' and a British poster of the times showed a glamorous woman chatting to some soldiers with the caption 'keep mum, she's not so dumb'. In the USA, Japanese Americans (but not German Americans) were interned for fear of sabotage or spying for the enemy. Those who supported internment pointed out that the proof of its success lay in the fact that no spying or sabotage ever took place.

However, we will never know if internment prevented any sabotage as most Japanese Americans, like Italian and German British, were never given the opportunity to prove their loyalty.

In Europe spies found it relatively easy to operate since there were thousands of displaced persons living in areas or countries where they were strangers. People from all over occupied Europe were drafted into factories far from their homes, most Jews were sent to Poland and ordinary people moved their families to places they thought were safer. This made it easier for British agents or local people to infiltrate sensitive areas and pass on information. However, many underground groups that contacted the British authorities were later discovered to have been double agents who arranged air drops of men and weapons only to hand them straight over to the authorities. In Germany communist groups

A French War Ministry poster from 1945 warns: 'Be Quiet! The German has fled; the spy remains.'

weblinks

For information on women spies, go to
www.waylinks.co.uk/worldwars homefront

such as the 'Red Orchestra' established radio contact with Soviet Intelligence and passed limited amounts of secret information to them.

Britain was very isolated when war broke out and it would have been difficult for spies to operate without arousing suspicion. The few dozen German spies who did enter the country quickly gave themselves away by carrying huge suitcases with clumsy radio equipment inside or, in one case, trying to order a beer in a pub at 9 a.m., hours before the sale of alcohol was legal. Some spies became double agents and one in particular, a Spaniard whose code name was Garbo, managed to help convince the German authorities that the landing for D-Day was the Pas de Calais rather than Normandy. This gave Allied troops time to make a successful landing before German reinforcements could arrive in Normandy.

The first German spy caught behind Allied lines, is executed by American soldiers in April 1945.

Loss of Freedom

For most people, war resulted in a loss of individual freedoms. In occupied countries there were curfews, identity cards, new laws regulating civilian behaviour, restrictions on where people could go, what they could say, listen to, read, write, buy, where they could work, who they could speak to or assist. Civilians in free countries often experienced similar restrictions, although to a lesser degree. In Britain much that was written in newspapers or broadcast on the radio was censored by the government. Private letters were also censored and the government had the power to tap telephone calls.

Japanese civilians remained totally isolated from the outside world for most of the war. Their government was, and always had been, very autocratic. For decades before the war Japanese secondary school children were taught the doctrine of total loyalty to the family and the state. With the outbreak of war this belief became even more important. Neighbourhood watch groups and the local police made the voicing of disagreement with government policies impossible. Anyone who dared to criticize the war would almost certainly be arrested.

Although many civilians had their freedom curbed by their own government, Allied propaganda focused on the idea that the Western forces were fighting for the freedom of all. Here an American war poster shows a Jew, a Catholic and a Protestant fighting together for religious freedom.

The silent column

In June 1940 the British government launched a 'silent column' campaign that encouraged citizens to inform on neighbours who were spreading rumours or speaking against the war. The public response was one of great resentment: Dorothy L. Sayers, a writer, summed it up:

'We have been shown a very faint glimpse of the things that we have been fighting against and now that we have seen it, we know for certain that we hate it beyond all imagination. To distrust our fellows, to become spies on them, to betray them to the law, to go in continual dumb terror for fear they should spy on us — that is the thing that Nazi government means and it is a thing we will not endure.'

Quoted in Stuart Hilton *Their Darkest Hour, The Hidden History of the Home Front 1939-45*, Sutton, 2001.

Similarly, in Germany individuals who spoke out against government policy were arrested and towards the end of the war could be executed.

In the case of Italy, civilian discontent with conscription, food shortages and bombing finally resulted in the fall of the dictator Benito Mussolini. The Fascist leader had ruled the country for twenty-one years, but by 1943 even his supporters realized that he had asked too much of the Italian people. During a meeting to decide Mussolini's future, one member of the Grand Fascist Council cried: 'In this war, we already have a hundred thousand dead, and we have a hundred thousand mothers who cry: "Mussolini has assassinated my son!"'. While Italians continued to experience loss of freedom, especially under the Nazi occupation of northern Italy, the degree of unhappiness amongst the general population was the driving force in bringing Mussolini's regime to an end.

CHAPTER FIVE:
Hardships

Food and Rationing

By the middle of the war most people in occupied Europe were living on a diet of 1,500 calories a day, barely enough to survive. Luxuries such as coffee and fresh fruit disappeared altogether and even basic foods such as milk, potatoes and bread were strictly rationed. Despite rationing, there were often barely enough essential supplies to provide people with their allocation of food.

In the USSR people began to starve while France, Holland and Italy fared worse than countries in Eastern Europe. In France a complex series of categories gave different rations to different groups. Small children were allowed extra milk and vitamins, workers in essential industries were permitted more calories and the elderly were considered not to need milk at all. In Italy rationing began in 1939 with restrictions on coffee, bread and pasta, and sales of meat restricted to five days a week. A black market developed and prices rose to about eight times their legal level. By 1942 even factory workers were struggling on 1,000 calories a day. In Japan luxury goods were prohibited, sugar was banned, and on one day a month citizens were forced to eat even less than they usually had in order to support the war effort. As in many other countries people had to turn to the black market in order to survive.

A German poster encouraging people not to waste food by throwing it away.

In Britain there were food shortages and butter, bacon, meat of all kinds and eggs were rationed. Although most people suffered minor hardships, the poorest people in Britain ate better during the war than they had before it began. Unemployment had reached record levels during the 1930s but with the outbreak of war most of the unemployed found work in war industries or the military. As a result, they could afford more food. Furthermore, unlike in peacetime, the government took measures to make sure that people ate reasonably well. In the USA petrol was rationed in order to preserve rubber and later in the war twenty essential items of food were rationed, including sugar, meat and coffee. There were very few real hardships however and higher wages meant that most people ate better during the war than they had previously.

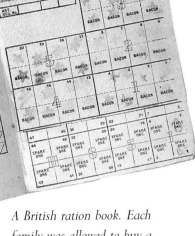

A British ration book. Each family was allowed to buy a limited quantity of several scarce products such as milk and meat. Most of these items were also available on the black market, sold at high prices without marking the buyer's ration card.

A rationed diet

This boy from the north of England remembers the strange food he was given because of rationing:

'We never starved, but we ate some ... funny things. Best was American dried egg. You poured a thick trickle into the frying pan, then as it cooked it blew up like a balloon, till it was two inches thick, like a big yellow hump backed whale. And we had whale meat ... there was so much of it — great big ... steaks as big as your plate ... we didn't care what it tasted like.'

Quoted in Stuart Hilton *Their Darkest Hour, The Hidden History of the Home Front 1939-45,* Sutton, 2001.

CIVIL DEFENCE

WOMEN WANTED FOR
EVACUATION SERVICE

OFFER YOUR SERVICES
TO YOUR LOCAL COUNCIL
OR ANY BRANCH OF WOMEN'S VOLUNTARY SERVICES

NATIONAL
SERVICE

A British government poster early in the war asks women to volunteer to help with the evacuation of children to the countryside. People who took on children from the cities received ten shillings (fifty pence) a week for the first child's upkeep and eight shillings and sixpence (forty two pence) for any others.

Children on the Home Front

War was often tedious for children in America and Britain. For the first time their mothers were at work and they had no active part to play in the war effort. In Britain a mass evacuation programme began almost as soon as war was declared. Over 1.5 million children took part in the initial evacuation, which aimed to place children in areas that would not be the target of enemy bombs. Some children were sent to stay with relatives in the countryside, but many more were billeted with strangers. What emerges from that period is the shock felt by country people at the condition of the children from working class areas — many were thin and unhealthy, had infections and were dressed in filthy, worn out clothes.

Over half of the children evacuated were reclaimed by their mothers within six months, partly because the expected air raids did not begin until the following summer and partly because the children found it impossible to settle in their new homes. In America children were affected by the enormous migrations that took place as people shifted to areas where war work was required. For the first time America experienced 'latch-key' children whose mothers went out to work. Juvenile delinquency rose 20 per cent during the war.

In Japan children were taught that commitment to their country and the war took precedence over everything. By 1943 all schools conducted compulsory martial arts training so that in the event of invasion children could defend themselves. For part of each day school students were sent to work on the harvest or in factories producing war materials. Once they reached the age of seventeen, boys were called into the armed forces. As Germany began to lose the war boys as young as fifteen were drafted into the armed forces.

The Kindertransport

Of all the children whose lives were scarred by World War II, Jewish children suffered the greatest deprivations. Before the war began about 9,000 German Jewish children were brought to Britain on the *kindertransport,* most of them never to see their parents again. They were housed in old army barracks or found homes with British Jewish families. Others with family in the USA or Canada escaped, but by 1941 Hitler had closed the borders and refused to allow any more Jews to leave. Of those that were trapped with their families in Europe, most died either in the ghettos of Eastern Europe of starvation or disease or in the gas chambers of the death camps – only adults survived the initial selections. In total, approximately 1.5 million children died because they were Jewish.

weblinks

For more information on the *kindertransport,* go to **www.waylinks.co.uk/worldwars homefront**

Munich, Germany, Autumn 1945. These survivors of the Allied bombing of the city search among the ruins for useful things such as wood for winter fuel.

CHAPTER SIX

Foreigners

On Foreign Soil

At any one time in World War II there were millions of displaced persons living outside their home country or region. Millions of people fled eastwards across the Soviet Union in advance of the German army. Millions more were transported by the Germans to slave labour, death or concentration camps. Thousands fled Burma in 1942 when the Japanese invaded and thousands of Jews fled from one temporary safe haven to another as the Germans advanced.

In Britain there were about 60,000 refugees who had fled the Hitler regime. As the war broke they and all other foreign nationals, including about 20,000 Italian foreign workers living in Britain, were examined for their potential as enemies of the state. They lived under a curfew and were not allowed to own radios, maps or any vehicles. Foreign nationals were sacked from their jobs even if their country was neutral. Mr Speer of Maidenhead (the son of a naturalized German) fought against Germany during World War I but his neighbours petitioned the government to sack him from his job of air raid warden. By May 1940 fear of a 'fifth column' in Britain had reached such a fever point that an order was given to arrest and intern all potentially dangerous foreigners. Attacks were made against Italian restaurants and police had to break up anti-Italian riots. Gracie Fields, a famous English singer, had to flee to the USA before she and her Italian husband became part of the round up of dangerous aliens. Later, German prisoners of war were brought to Britain to work clearing the streets of bomb damage or working on the land. Some were adopted by British families or local church groups who felt sorry for them being alone and far from their families. Such groups organized Christmas parties and visits to British homes during public holidays, and some kept in contact with the prisoners after the war had ended.

'Aliens' who have been rounded up by police fill sacks with straw for their beds. They have been interned in a newly-built housing estate in Liverpool.

American troops are pictured here enjoying their rations as they arrive in England.

GIs

American troops billeted in Britain were generally admired by the population for their brimming good health, vast quantities of rationed goods and their unfamiliar manners. For hundreds of young girls living far from home to work in munitions factories, putting on a dance for the GIs was a public duty and great fun as well. Many transatlantic marriages occurred during the war. For some Britons, black American servicemen were the first black people they had ever seen. Attitudes ranged from shock at the segregation and discrimination in the American armed forces to home-grown racial prejudice at these well-paid and lively men having a good time in British dance halls and pubs.

Minority Groups in the USA

In the USA a similar fear of 'the enemy within' became apparent. At the outbreak of World War II, America had a population of 127,000 Japanese Americans. Many had become American citizens and some had never set foot in Japan. There were also about 900,000 German and Italian citizens or recent arrivals living in the USA.

After the bombing of Pearl Harbor in 1941, 112,000 Japanese, mostly from the west coast of America, were given a few days' notice and then interned in detention camps. These camps were hastily constructed out of wood and tar paper in desert areas that were subject to extremes of weather and dust storms. Although families were allowed to remain together, they lived in cramped, insanitary conditions with few toilet facilities and no cooking facilities. Inmates had to pay for meals prepared in mess halls. The barracks were fenced and guarded by armed troops in watch towers. Many people had no time to sell their homes or businesses and it is estimated that about $400 million worth of property and possessions were lost. No other ethnic groups were treated in this way and insult was added to injury by conscripting interned Japanese American men. Those who refused

Armed troops guard these Japanese Americans being taken to an internment camp. In the USA families were allowed to stay together while in Canada the men were separated from their families.

weblinks ‣

For more information on the internment of Japanese Americans on the west coast of the USA after 1941 go to
www.waylinks.co.uk/worldwars homefront

to be drafted faced prison sentences, which meant they were unable to look after their families in the internment camps. In fact, many Japanese Americans willingly enlisted and two Japanese American battalions served in Italy. They were among the most highly decorated of American servicemen.

African and Mexican Americans also experienced problems during the war. At the time many states had discriminatory employment and social laws and African Americans who were conscripted were placed in segregated units and excluded from the marines and air corps. At first they were also excluded from war industries. However, by 1941 African Americans were vital to the war industry and 1.8 million black people migrated to the northern states to work in factories there. In Los Angeles in 1943 there were racist attacks against young Mexican American factory workers, which came to be known as the 'zoot suit riots' after their distinctive style of dressing.

Japanese Americans

In all, 120,313 Japanese Americans were interned; 5,918 were born in the camps to imprisoned parents; 1,579 were sent to camps where they were put to work in the fields; 1,118 were taken from Hawaii; and 219, mostly non-Japanese husbands or wives, entered voluntarily.

When internment ended 54,127 Japanese Americans returned to the West Coast; 52,798 moved to inland states; 4,724 moved to Japan; 3,121 remained in internment camps; 2,355 joined the armed forces; 1,862 had died during imprisonment; 1,322 were sent to prisons; and four were classified as unauthorized departures, that is, they escaped.

The Russian Gulags

In the USSR there were mass arrests and deportations of ethnic minorities. Chechens and Karachi from the Caucasus who had rebelled against Russian authority before the Germans had invaded were deported to labour camps (gulags) in the north of the Soviet Union. Thousands died *en route* and more died in the camps. Kalmyks, Ingush, Balkars and Crimean Tartars, all strong ethnic groups within the Soviet Union who had remained loyal to their own country, were also sent to the gulags because they were considered potential enemies. An estimated 2.5 million Soviet citizens were placed in such camps.

CHAPTER SEVEN:
Changed Lives

Germany and Japan

At the end of the war, the civilians of the three Axis powers found their countries occupied by Allied forces. Their lives were reduced to the most primitive level. Japan's cities were devastated, millions were homeless, starving and suffering from the effects of the two atomic bombs. Most means of transport were destroyed, no food was entering the cities and few people were able to make their way into the countryside to find food. The Japanese also had the humiliation of watching their wartime leaders face trial for war crimes. In Okinawa, thousands of people had committed suicide during the US invasion and American troops had had little choice but to watch as people threw themselves off cliffs. Once the war was over some Japanese were so distressed by the fall of their empire that they, too, considered suicide.

An elderly woman, her daughter and grandchild leave the devastation of Hiroshima with a cart of their belongings.

Germany was divided between the occupying powers, its cities destroyed, its people near starvation. In the final weeks of the war thousands of people had been executed by their own government for deserting their posts or talking of surrender. There were terrible stories about the treatment of German civilians by Russian troops entering Germany.

Germany quickly became a pawn in the struggle for power between the Western Allies and the USSR. The Western powers wanted a friendly pro-West country in central Europe while the USSR wanted a communist state as a barrier between itself and the West. A beaten and subjugated Germany was of no use to either side and aid was quickly provided to help rebuild the German economy and German cities. Trials of war criminals followed later but few of the people who had committed war crimes ever faced justice.

A year after the war had ended there were still food shortages and homelessness all over Europe. This photograph was taken in Hamburg in August 1946.

The Homeless

In the immediate aftermath of World War II, 60 million people were homeless. The majority, 40 million, of these were in China as a result of Japanese actions. As countries in Europe were liberated from German occupation, they began expelling ethnic Germans from their territory with little concern for what would happen to them. 400,000 ethnic Germans from Hungary and Yugoslavia, 110,000 from Romania and 2.5 million from Czechoslovakia were made homeless. Four million Germans fled Poland ahead of the invading Russian troops. In all about twelve million Germans were deported or interned after the war and about two million died in the process.

Europe's Jews

The rest of Europe experienced similar chaos and destruction of the means of survival. In Holland the retreating German troops opened the gates of the dams and a sizeable amount of land was flooded. As well as physical discomforts, French people had to deal with the thousands of their own citizens who had collaborated with Germany. In Eastern Europe there was also chaos.

However, throughout Europe most civilians knew that although they faced months or even years of terrible hardships, eventually they would be able to rebuild their shattered cities and continue with their lives. This was not so for Europe's Jewish population. As the war progressed the Nazis had systematically deported and murdered whole Jewish communities from all over Europe. At the end of the war the few thousands of sick and starving Jewish people who remained alive in the concentration and death camps had been forced to march to Germany to avoid the liberating Soviet troops. Thousands died on the marches either from exhaustion or by execution. On arrival in Germany they were abandoned in the remaining camps to await liberation by Allied troops. Of those that survived many more died when horrified Allied troops tried to help them with food that was too rich for their weakened systems. Many survivors returned to their home countries to find their homes occupied by one-time neighbours, their families lost and their possessions looted. In parts of Poland, Jews who had survived the ghettos, camps and death marches struggled home only to be murdered when they arrived. Other survivors were given visas to settle in the USA or Britain while many demanded the right to settle in Palestine.

The Theodor Herzl, *carrying 2,700 Jewish illegal immigrants to Palestine, April 1947. The British Royal Navy boarded the ship before it reached Palestine. In the battle for control of the vessel, two Jewish survivors of the Holocaust were killed and twenty were injured.*

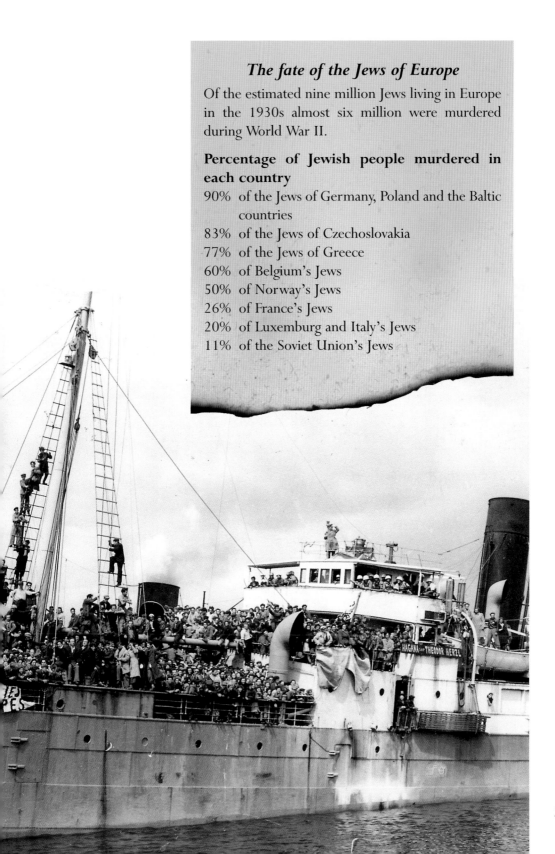

The fate of the Jews of Europe

Of the estimated nine million Jews living in Europe in the 1930s almost six million were murdered during World War II.

Percentage of Jewish people murdered in each country

90% of the Jews of Germany, Poland and the Baltic countries
83% of the Jews of Czechoslovakia
77% of the Jews of Greece
60% of Belgium's Jews
50% of Norway's Jews
26% of France's Jews
20% of Luxemburg and Italy's Jews
11% of the Soviet Union's Jews

The Soviet Union

When Soviet citizens stepped outside to celebrate VE (Victory in Europe) day in 1945 they had yet to add up the cost of that victory. Eleven million Soviet soldiers had died. Seven million civilians had lost their lives. The vast majority of people had lost their homes or family members or their jobs. By 1959 only two-thirds of women of marriageable age who survived were married because so many young men had died. A third of houses, factories and farms were destroyed. Untold amounts of wealth that could have been spent on creating a peaceful state had instead been spent on financing the war.

Many Soviet citizens continued to go hungry and experience unemployment for decades after the end of the war. Instead of reaching a profitable and peaceful relationship with their wartime allies, the Soviet Union became embroiled in the Cold War – building newer and bigger weapons became more important than reconstruction. The communist dictator, Stalin, was more powerful than he had been before the war and any chance of a more liberal government coming to power was lost.

Russia, 1945. A woman welcomes her husband home from the war.

Smaller Eastern European countries were to become Soviet states standing as a barrier between the USSR and the threat of invasion from the West. Many Soviets saw war and the military as the means of keeping the USSR safe and the war experience justified the cruel treatment of collaborators and minority groups.

The German troops left little behind them as they retreated into Germany. Here Soviet villagers are picking through some waste looking for food.

Destruction in the Soviet Union

This official report made in 1945 gives some idea of the devastation that people had to cope with in 1945:

'The German-fascist invaders completely or partially destroyed and burnt 1,710 towns and settlements and more than 70,000 villages and hamlets; burnt and destroyed more than six million buildings and rendered homeless about 25 million people; destroyed 31,580 industrial enterprises, decommissioned [put out of action] metal works which before the war yielded 60 per cent of the steel, and mines which yielded more than 60 per cent of the coal in the country; destroyed 65,000 kilometres of railway lines and 4,100 stations; destroyed and looted tens of thousands of collective and state farms, slaughtered, seized or drove back to Germany 7 million horses, 17 million cattle, 20 million pigs, 27 million sheep and goats. In addition they destroyed and looted 40,000 hospitals ... 84,000 schools... and 43,000 public libraries.'

John Barber and Mark Harrison, *The Soviet Home Front, a Social and Economic History of the USSR in World War II*, Longman, 1991.

The Channel Islands were occupied by Nazi troops from June 1940 until May 1945. By 1944 German supply lines were cut and both the civilian population and the occupying troops were suffering from serious food shortages. This house expresses the feelings of the islanders when liberation finally came.

Post-war Britain

During the war about 100,000 British civilians had been killed and a quarter of a million Britons were injured. 264,000 soldiers never returned to their families. Some of those that did return had spent years in prisoner of war camps under inhuman conditions. For other men war had been a life-changing experience. The army had provided for all their needs for five years and returning to bills, run-down homes, rationed food, troubled families and boring desk jobs was extremely challenging. The cities were in ruins, many people were homeless and rationing was still in place. People had endured nightly bombing attacks and thousands had suppressed terrible emotional damage simply because they could not afford to give in to their suffering. Many children had spent the war years living in the countryside away from their families and had adapted to their new lives. Like their fathers, some of these children found returning to the city and their families as difficult as leaving had been.

Many women who had done a great deal for the war effort, working in factories, as air raid wardens or in voluntary organizations, returned to their role of housewife, looking after the children as the nursery schools closed and the men returned to take their places in industry. Having been the breadwinner and head of the household for several years, women were suddenly expected to return to their domestic duties and give up their new-found independence. For thousands of people the difficulties involved in the sudden return to peace were too great. The divorce rate rose by 50 per cent in Britain in the years after the war.

Rebuilding damaged cities was a financial drain on the British government in the post-war years. Here workers clear a bomb site in Cannon Street, London.

The Welfare State

After the war a new Labour government quickly came to power in Britain and preparations for the Welfare State began. The war had exposed poor living conditions in the cities, inadequate wages and health care and huge social inequalities. These were no longer acceptable to people who felt they had contributed to their country's survival. The Welfare State promised health care, education and at least enough money for everyone's basic needs. Many historians have suggested that it was the experience of war, the evacuations and the demands of the poor people who had contributed to the war effort that brought this about. Others have suggested that most of the welfare reforms would have taken place anyway, or even earlier if the war had not happened.

Post-War America

Distant from the theatres of war, Americans did not experience much of what went on in Europe and Asia. In 1945 most of the world emerged from war with their economies damaged and their citizens traumatized. For some Americans the war was 'the most popular war in American history' as the historian John P. Diggins has suggested. Wages rose, unemployment came to an end, social barriers began to break down and America was on the winning side of what was seen as a clear-cut battle between good and evil. The war had an enormous effect on the lives of American citizens, especially America's ethnic minorities and women. One historian, Tony Badger, has claimed that the war was 'the juggernaut that ran over American society' because it brought about such enormous changes.

Many Americans remember the war for the way it brought a sense of togetherness to a divided society. African Americans had demonstrated their worth to society. By 1946 there was a Commission on Civil Rights in place and President Truman condemned race violence the following year. Segregation in the armed forces and the civil service came to an end by 1948. Six years later segregation in schools was prohibited.

The position of women was similar to British women. Needed for war work, they were encouraged to find jobs but when the men returned thousands of women were laid off. Suddenly it was their patriotic duty to return to the home. But for many people, drained by the war effort and separation from their families this was welcome. The marriage and birth rates rose, the feared economic slump didn't take place, thousands of ex-servicemen used their readjustment pay to go to college or buy businesses and homes and America quickly became an affluent society.

In the USA people's concerns turned to their families as life went back to the familiar things – a simple meal, settling into a new job, getting to know the family again.

weblinks

For more information on post-war America, go to
www.waylinks.co.uk/worldwarshomefront

Settling down to married life

320,000 American servicemen died in the battlefields of World War II. For the eight million who did return the important goals were security and stability. Abroad the Cold War was under way and a new threat to stability came with it. Betty Friedan in *The Feminine Mystique* described the feelings of Americans:

'We were all vulnerable, homesick, lonely, frightened. A pent up hunger for marriage, home and children was felt simultaneously by several different generations, a hunger which in the prosperity of post-war America everyone could suddenly satisfy.'

Betty Friedan, *The Feminine Mystique*, New York, 1974.

Timeline

1937 Japanese troops invade China.

1939 **1 September** Germany invades Poland.
3 September Britain and France declare war on Germany.

1940 **April-June** Germany invades Norway, Denmark, the Netherlands, Belgium and France.
10 June Italy declares war on Britain and France.
September The Blitz begins. Japan invades Indo-China. Italy invades Egypt.
October Greece is invaded by Italy.

1941 **April** USA agrees to lend weapons to Britain. USA becomes the 'arsenal of democracy'. Germany invades Yugoslavia.
May Crete becomes a war zone as Allied and German troops fight.
22 June Operation Barbarossa – the German invasion of the USSR brings more Eastern European countries into the war zones. Thousands of Jews are murdered.
October The Siege of Leningrad begins.
7 December Japan bombs Pearl Harbor. The USA enters the war. Japanese troops invade Malaya.
8 December USA and Britain declare war on Japan.
11 December Germany declares war on the USA.

1942 **February** Singapore falls to the Japanese. Massacres of Chinese civilians. Darwin, Australia is bombed.

June Japanese conquer the Philippines.

1943 **July** Allied bombs cause a firestorm in Hamburg.
September Italy is occupied by both German and Allied troops.
November Japanese and US troops fight in the Solomon Islands.

1944 **January** The Siege of Leningrad ends. US and Japanese troops fight in the Marshall Islands.
February India is briefly invaded by Japan.
June American troops take Saipan. Japan is now accessible to bomber planes. Russian troops begin to drive German forces back through the western Soviet Union. Allied troops land in France and move through civilian populations driving German troops before them.
August The Warsaw Uprising in which thousands of civilians die.

1945 **January** Russian troops liberate Warsaw.
February Allied bombing raid on Dresden.
March Firebomb attacks on Tokyo.
April US troops land in Okinawa. Mass panic in civilian population. Berlin falls to the Russians.
8 May VE Day.
6 August Atomic bomb dropped on Hiroshima.
9 August Atomic bomb dropped on Nagasaki.
15 August Victory over Japan Day.
2 September Japan surrenders.

Glossary

air raid an attack by enemy aircraft releasing bombs.

Allies countries that fought in World War II against Germany, Japan and their allies.

anti-Semitic discriminating against and hating Jewish people.

Aryan the Nazis used this term to mean a white person, not Jewish, gypsy or Slavic in origin. They believed Aryans were members of a superior race that the Jews were trying to corrupt.

autocratic an unelected government that holds absolute power over its citizens.

auxiliary nurses women who had been partly trained in nursing and who helped the qualified nurses.

Auxiliary Territorial Service the branch of the army into which women were conscripted.

auxiliary units organized groups that supported the army's work.

Axis The alliance between Germany, Japan and Italy against the Allies.

billet to provide someone with a temporary home in war time.

black marketeering selling rationed food or luxuries at a high price.

Blitz the German bombing campaign against Britain that began in 1940.

carpet bombing bombing a wide area such as a whole city rather than a specific target such as a factory or army base.

Chechens a minority group of Soviet citizens.

civil defence protecting a country's civilians and property from within the country.

civilians ordinary citizens who are not part of the armed services.

concentration camps camps where certain groups of people could be isolated and confined.

conscription the compulsory call up for the armed forces or for work in war industries.

curfew a set time at which citizens had to be inside their homes, shops and businesses had to close and no-one was allowed to walk the streets.

death camps camps built in Poland for the specific purpose of murdering people.

D-Day short for Deliverance Day, the invasion of northern France by the Allies in June 1944.

displaced persons people who have been removed from or fled their homes.

doctrine an idea which is taught to members of a group or society.

evacuation the organized removal of groups of people from an area of danger.

Fascists people who believe that their country or race is more important than anything and who support a powerful controlling government, often a dictator which does not allow any opposition.

family allowance a small weekly pension given to families with children of school age.

fifth column a term first used in the Spanish Civil War to describe a secret army within the enemy country, which was ready to take up arms when the opportunity presented itself. In Britain people feared that Germans and Italians living in Britain might have formed such a secret force.

ghettos enclosed and run down areas of a city or town where Jews were forced to live.

gulags labour camps in the USSR.

incendiary bombs bombs designed to create fires rather than to explode.

Land Army a mostly voluntary group of about 80,000 women who moved to the countryside to work on the farms during the war.

latch-key children those children whose mothers worked during the day and who were not at home to let the children in when they came home from school.

lebensraum living space – the extra territory that the Nazi government felt that Germans needed if they were to become more powerful.

liberation the moment when the armies of a friendly government move into a country and drive out the occupying forces.

nationalistic an idea or a gesture supporting one's country.

Nazi ideology the belief that Aryan people such as the Germans were of a superior race and were justified in treating other races as inferior.

neighbourhood watch a voluntary scheme where local people carry out surveillance of the factories and houses in their neighbourhood. In wartime they would have been looking for looters, or small fires caused by incendiary bombs during an air raid.

occupied countries countries that have foreign governments ruling them against the wishes of the citizens.

occupying forces the troops of a foreign government which has attacked and taken power.

partisan a small and often secret force whose objective is to make swift raids or attacks against an enemy.

Pearl Harbor a naval base and the headquarters of the US Pacific fleet in Hawaii. It is also the name given to the attack on the USA by Japan, which resulted in the USA entering the war.

phoney war the months following Britain's declaration of war against Germany in 1939 when there were no bombing raids and nothing seemed to be happening.

readjustment pay the grant that returning US servicemen were given in order to make it easier for them to settle back into civilian life.

segregation the forced isolation of a particular race of people by making them live, attend school, work or socialize only amongst themselves.

theatres of war the places in the world where the major battles took place.

untermenschen the word that Nazis used for races of people that they considered to be sub-human or of an inferior race to their own.

USSR abbreviation for the Union of Soviet Socialist Republics, dominated by Russia, which broke up at the end of the 1980s.

VE Day Victory in Europe Day, 8 May 1945, the day after Germany surrendered.

Welfare State a social welfare system introduced by the British government following World War II.

Sources and Resources

Further Reading

William Bird, Harry R. Rubenstein, William L. Bird, *Design for Victory: World War II Posters on the American Home Front*, Princeton Architectural Press, 1998.

Penny Colman, *Rosie the Riveter: Women's Work on the Home Front in World War II*, Crown Publishing Group, 1998.

Frances Fyfield, *The Home Front*, Heinemann Library, 1995.

Bonnie Hinman, Bonnie Harvey, Adam Wallenta, *The Home Front*, Barbour Publications, 1999.

Fiona Reynoldson, *The Home Front: The Blitz,* Hodder Wayland, 2002.

Fiona Reynoldson, *The Home Front: Evacuation*, Hodder Wayland, 2002.

Fiona Reynoldson, *The Home Front: Rationing*, Hodder Wayland, 1993.

Fiona Reynoldson, *The Home Front: The Women's War*, Hodder Wayland, 1993.

Stewart Ross, *At Home in World War 2: The Blitz*, Evans Brothers Limited, 2002.

Stewart Ross, *At Home in World War 2: Evacuation*, Evans Brothers Limited, 2002.

Stewart Ross, *At Home in World War 2: Rationing*, Evans Brothers Limited, 2002.

Stewart Ross, *At Home in World War 2: Women's War*, Evans Brothers Limited, 2002.

Ann Stalcup, *On the Home Front*, Shoestring Publications, 1998.

Other Sources

John Barber and Mark Harrison, *The Soviet Home Front, a Social and Economic History of the USSR in World War II*, Longman, 1991.

Earl R. Beck, *Under the Bombs The German Home Front 1942-1945*, University Press of Kentucky, 1986.

Lucy S. Dawidowicz, *The War Against the Jews*, Penguin, 1990.

Frank Gibney (ed.), *Senso – The Japanese Remember the Pacific War: Letters to the Editor of Asahi Shimbun*, East Gate, 1995.

Stuart Hylton, *Their Darkest Hour: The Hidden History of the Home Front 1939-1945*, Sutton, 2001.

Clive Ponting, *Armageddon,* Sinclair Stevenson, 1995.

Martin Kitchen, *Nazi Germany at War*, Longman, 1995.

Jeremy Noakes (ed.), *The Civilian in War The Home Front in Europe, Japan and the USA in World War II*, University of Exeter Press, 1992.

Raynes Minns, *Bombers and Mash: the Domestic Front 1939-45*, Virago, 1980.

For further information on topics relevant to this book go to:
www.waylinks.co.uk/worldwarshomefront

Index

If a number is in **bold** type, there is an illustration.